PRESSBOOKS
Simple Book Production

THE BUSINESS OF PRIVATE INVESTIGATION

RISK6

The Business of Private Investigation

Contents

Introduction 1

1. Chapter 1- Getting Started-Let's grow 5

2. Chapter 2- Hiring and Firing in a Crazy Industry
.... 24

3. Chapter 3- Sales and Marketing 35

4. Chapter 4- Business Administration 41

5. Chapter 5- Investigative Products 52

6. Chapter 6- Investigative Reports 70

7. Chapter 7- Database Search Companies 79

8. Chapter 8- Equipment 85

9. Chapter 9- Internet Presence 90

10. Chapter 10- Investigative Library 96

Introduction

Hello, My name is Barry Maguire and I live in the Metropolitan Boston, Massachusetts area. I started my business New England Risk Management Investigations Inc in 2001. Prior to that, I worked as a staff investigator-supervisor for several private investigation companies. I have conducted or supervised more than 5,000 investigations to date. I have hired and fired dozens of investigators and support staff. During this time frame, I've learned a lot of lessons, most the hard way. I hope that I can guide you around some of the potholes and pitfalls that I sped toward and through as I grew my business.

The reason I wrote this book is simple. I wish something similar was available to me prior to starting my investigations company in 2001.

I'm sure some of the information I provide today was available back then, however, you must remember that the internet was still in its infancy. Apple had just introduced its *first* iPod and Napster (you remember Napster, right?) reached 26 million downloads. So, yes the information may have been somewhere on the burgeoning internet, but I would have certainly saved myself thousands of dollars if all of the information was centrally located.

Looking back I often wished that there was a sort of "how-to" manual to start a PI firm. I definitely read whatever books and magazine articles I could get my hands on, but to say that there was a dearth of readily available information would be an understatement. So after many years, I thought I'd write the book that I undoubtedly needed at the beginning of my career.

I intentionally crafted this book to be easily consumed, (perhaps on surveillance?) with short and distinct chapters, describing what *I* believe are best business decisions and practices. The target audience for this book is those contemplating or just beginning their own journey into the world of private investigation business ownership. I wish you well on the voyage and I sincerely hope this book will save you time and a few dollars. Godspeed!

1

Chapter 1-
Getting Started-Let's grow

Congratulations! you've made the decision to open your own investigations business. I'm willing to bet you won't regret it. Well, first things first, what will your corporate structure look like? How will you invoice your client and most importantly how will you get paid?

Business structures When starting out please take the opportunity to choose the appropriate corporate structure. The two main business entities are the S Corp and the LLC limited liability corporation. According to biz filing.com, both the S Corp and the LLC are pass-through tax entities, and while the S corps must file a business tax return, LLC only file business tax returns if the LLC has more than one owner with pass through taxations, no income taxes are paid at the business level. Business profit or losses passed through to the owner's personal tax return. LLC are also allowed to have business subsidiaries while and S Corp does have limitations. You can definitely use one of the online business formation companies such as legal zoom or biz filings, however, if you'd like to save some money take the time to walk down to your local secretary of state's office and have them walk you through it, they can't deny you since that's what they get paid to do. The secretary of state's corporation office is cheaper and you already pay them through your tax dollars, make them earn it for once and take the saving and go to a nice lunch!

Tip: Don't go to the Secretary of State's office on a Monday or a Friday. You'll get a more helpful state employee midweek

Self-employment tax

S Corporations may have preferable self-employment taxes compared to the LC because the owner can be treated as an employer. All in all I believe that the LLC is probably best for most investigative agencies, however in some states all officials or officers of the corporation are required to qualify for the agency/investigative license. Please check with your licensing authority prior to deciding on your business structure. There are several online companies that will incorporate your business for you including bizfilings.com and legalzoom.com. Potential business owners can also simply take advantage of your secretary of state's office. They can walk you through the paperwork and best of all it is usually cheaper (by hundreds of dollars) to do it in person. Let the state help you rather than just take your hard-earned tax dollars.Don't' go to the incorporation office on a Monday morning or Friday afternoon (especially in the summer months.)

Bookkeeping

Book keeping for business has never been easier. The main hurdle is setting up your system. I'd strongly recommend hiring a bookkeeper to set up your initial data entry for your accounting program, I did not do this when first starting out and it was a headache. Also, have your bookkeeper review the program at least quarterly. Getting accurate cash flow data is imperative to an investigative startup. I would highly recommend an online accounting program. We have used QuickBooks online for more than a decade. QuickBooks is the most used accounting software in the world, so most accountants and bookkeepers are familiar with it. We use the online version rather than the boxed program. If you use QuickBooks online your bookkeeper or accountant can log on from anywhere to work on your books. There is also peachtree accounting software. I am not as familiar with this program but it is worth a look just for the sake of comparison.

Some of the things I wish I had known prior to opening my own shop Stress

Actually I knew going in, that it would be stressful, I just didn't know to what degree. The constant pressure to get results can be torturous. Results, once obtained immediately become your client's success, only failure is yours to keep in this business. The adjuster or lawyer is the hero when it was you who drove from your house (without shovelling your driveway) when it was completely dark out, In order to obtain hours of video of a claimant snow blowing. It is the genius of the insurance company S.I.U. representative that shown through when you were the one who overcame the incorrect address and description, in order to confirm the claimant is working at a new gym. Can you handle that type of slight time and again? The only reward you will receive is getting your invoice paid within ninety days. Know these facts before you jump into this crazy business.

Private investigation is lucrative

The previous paragraph on stress may seem like I'm against becoming involved in the investigation industry, I'm not. There is an upside, several in fact. I've done pretty well on the income side of the ledger and I know others in my area have as well. Since 2002 my first full year of business, I've taken approximately 110,000 – 130,000 a year in salary. That does not include quarterly and biannual bonuses. Hard work does pay off in this business, but make sure you are aware of the cost in terms of work-life balance. Max out your pre-tax retirement contributions, you can thank me later!

Tip place 10% (Post-tax) of every paid invoice in a separate account, in twenty-some months you won't need to go to the bank for expansion funds.

Work-life balance

Simply, work-life balance at least for me has been difficult. The effects of eighty-hour weeks on a consistent basis are highly debilitating to body and mind. At various times I was fifteen to pounds overweight, I did not maintain friendships like I should have. The little free time I had was owed to my growing family.

During one very busy summer I worked surveillance for forty days straight without a day off. By the end of this cycle, I could simply not hold a thought in my head. I was forced to re-schedule surveillance and decompress by taking some time off. Guess what? the cases were still there when I returned and my clients barely noticed. Don't fall into this trap; I beg you, be good to yourself. You cannot serve from an empty vessel.

Below is a copy of an article I wrote for Pursuit Magazine, which illustrates my outlook on the investigations business.

It's not all surf and sunsets in this biz.

A Boston PI dispels a few myths about the world of private investigations. (hint: It's not as Ferrari- and helicopter-infested as you might think.)

A career in the private investigations field can be very rewarding.

The casework can be fascinating. You frequently work with extremely smart and interesting people. Mobile surveillance can be a blast. However, there are several stubborn myths that have attached themselves to the investigations industry.

Let's explore some of the myths and the (sometimes) harsh realities of being a real PI.

Myth: Boom! It's payday. All PIs are rolling in dough. Magnum had a helicopter and a Ferrari 308 GTS!

Reality: The vast majority of investigators are simply working stiffs. They run a sole proprietorship or have a single partner or employee. Sure, we have what some consider a high billable rate, between $60-100 hourly, but what newcomers fail to recognize is that we do NOT get to keep all that cash. Not even close.

Usually there is an effective corporate-personal tax rate of about 46%. Shocked? Don't be. Add in liability insurance and arcane bonding requirements, and you'll have a very little leftover for hiring T.C. to fly the helicopter.

We are working stiffs—that is the reality. Skip the Ferrari and focus on the 401K. You can do very well financially; just know that you EARN every penny.

And by the way, as I'm sure you'll recall, the Ferrari wasn't Magnum's in the first place. Neither was the chopper or the beachfront estate.

Myth: A "real" private investigator? How exciting! You conduct surveillance and use spy cameras? You must be like James Bond!

Reality: You are sitting on a subject's residence, on ten-hour surveillance shifts. Midway through the second shift, at around noon, the subject finally ventures out to collect her mail. Thrilling, right?

Nope. It's not. But this the game. You'll have some excitement certainly. However, there are many days where recording a video of someone retrieving the mail is the highlight of your work day.

Do we need to talk about waiting in line at the court clerk's office? Yawn!

Myth: Do a great job, and your clients will be loyal.

Reality: The investigations industry is a fickle one. I have personally saved clients millions over the course of a contract, and suddenly, poof! They no longer take your calls. It may be for all sorts of reasons, and you may never know why they stop using your firm. It's the nature of the business.

If you need constant, positive reenforcement, this business is not for you. A paid invoice is usually your sole acknowledgment. Know that going in, and keep on plugging away.

Myth: My business focus is going to be "general public" clients. They are easier to deal with, and I can charge more for my services.

Reality: Members of the general public have a skewed view of what we do. Sometimes agonizingly so. They have no idea why we can't just tap someone's phone or break into a vehicle.

When you explain that you'd end up in prison if you complied with their requests, they're confused. I mean, they saw it on the "Rockford Files," so why can't you just...(insert felony).

A surprising number of people are also very difficult to deal with. Some are simply mentally and morally deficient. You'll meet your share of both. Always do your own due diligence on your client no matter whom they claim to be. Go ahead — charge that higher rate. You'll need it for aspirin, as you will have a great many headaches.

Myth: If I am the Sam Spade of my era, the world will beat a path to my door.

Reality: Investigative acumen, drive, and a cool hat are simply not enough in the digital age. You definitely need those characteristics, sans fedora, but you will also require a deep understanding of marketing, networking, and SEO strategies. You need to have a professional domain name and an optimized website. You'll want to be active in your state's PI association. You may even want to... (gulp) write an article for an investigations magazine!

Private investigation is a great career. I am not trying to dissuade you from joining our ranks — I simply want you to know what you're in for.

Deal in reality (you're just not going to have a helicopter!), and you'll have a gratifying and profitable career.

Licensing – Insurance – Bonding

In the United States, almost all private investigations licensing is handled at the state level. The few remaining states without state level licensing usually have a city or town procedure.

Typically the licensing follows an apprenticeship profile, meaning you work as an apprentice of sorts to a licensed investigator. The apprenticeship period is usually between three to five years. Some jurisdictions require a standardized test. Check your local requirements before you quit the apprenticeship!

Tip! If you have the bug to start your own investigation business during your "apprenticeship" period, keep it to yourself! a budding entrepreneur makes a lot of business owners nervous. They frequently see you as likely business competition, be alert for this mindset in a manager, it's a major red flag!

Depending on your state, the licensing authority can be a blessing or a curse. The seven states I've worked with have been both. Talk to members of your private investigations association to get an accurate picture of exactly what happens in your state.

I've found in most states that a felony conviction of any offense prohibits you from obtaining your own license or working for a licensed agency. The promulgating authority in most areas may excuse a misdemeanor record; however offenses involving fraud or "moral turpitude" will likely preclude you from working in the investigative field.

Insurance – General Liability

If you plan on working in the insurance investigation field you will be required to have minimum of one million dollar policy, three million for occurrence general liability policy. Some insurance carriers we've worked with require much more. I can recall raising our policy limits to five million. Many insurance companies will also require you to add their company as additionally insured. General liability policy can be tricky, the premiums increase according to your yearly revenue. The more you make the higher the premium. Make sure you are keenly aware of what is and what isn't covert under your general liability policy.

Personal disability-injury insurance

We do some pretty dangerous things in this business, frequent and fast driving, venturing into bad neighborhoods, spying on people. Get a personal injury policy, even if you are covered by worker's compensation insurance. If injured, worker's compensation policies only replace a percentage of your income, get a disability policy on top of that. You can thank me later.

Worker's comp insurance

In most states worker compensation is mandatory, however some states have an exemption for sole proprietors. The best way to deal with these sometimes confusing insurance issues is to find a good insurance agent, specializing in business insurance, they are usually cost-effective as well, as they get paid on commission from the insurance carriers.

Time to grow

Be ready for yes

Be watchful for one of the most surprising things that can swamp your budding investigative business, success!

We all plan for no, no I don't need your services, no we don't need another vendor, no we have staff investigators for that. What we are **not** ready for often times is **yes.**

If you are not ready for yes, it can kill your business. Success creates its own challenges. During the early 2000's we had been marketing the second largest insurance company in the world, to become a certified vendor for investigative services. We had experienced some success up to that point in marketing local worker's compensation carriers. We had three local carriers, however, we're always looking to grow. The national carrier approved our firm as a certified vendor in January of 2003. During our contract negotiations we were definitely informed that there would likely be a high volume of assignments coming in. This is exactly what we were looking to hear. We had assured our new client that we could without a doubt handle a high volume of workflow. We did meet our obligation to this client, however, I would be untruthful in saying that our level of service to our local clients did not suffer. On some level we felt privileged and excited to be placed on such a valuable vendor panel. Some may say that we were blinded by the bright shiny bauble placed in front of us. I would certainly agree with that statement, at least to a point. The national insurance company poured the work in and we began to hit home run after home run. We soon became the top vendor in the region. That alone prompted even more work to come in from this, now a very happy client. We were envisioning this client and other large clients to be our companies future. Subsequently, our commitment to our smaller local companies was reduced, not intentionally but at least subconsciously. I still feel bad about this, a management failure on my part, no doubt.

When I say our level of commitment fell off, I don't mean totally, we continued doing solid surveillance work, but case scheduling and client communication suffered, as our focus was on our new client. The billable hours from this client dwarfed what we were doing for our local clients, so I guess it was natural that they received our primary focus. As the months progressed the process continued. We were a valued vendor for one company, while an average vendor for our local clients, Then our national client asked if we could handle an even larger workload. We were being swamped by success and didn't even see it! By the end of that year we parted ways with two local clients, the parting was a mutual decision and best for our business, but I still feel I should have, could have saved this book of business with just a little more focus and delegation of resources. So remember be ready for yes, but success brings its own problems to the table!

2

Chapter 2-
Hiring and Firing in a Crazy Industry

Hiring and Firing in the PI Industry

Hiring employees in your investigative startup means you have achieved a measure of success, congratulations! Now focus on reality, employees in this business can be both a blessing and a curse. Be diligent in your hires, they can make you money or cost your thousands. Hire for what your business requires, don't try to hire your mirror image. Here's a newsflash your employees will never work as hard as you do, nor should they, its YOUR business!

Here is another article that I wrote for Pursuit Magazine in 2016 on hiring and firing employees. I believe it provides a primer on the employment process for this crazy business we've chosen. Check it out!

Let's face it: Hiring for the private investigation field is ... different. We are an atypical industry that requires workers to perform atypical tasks. We are basically asking candidates to cast aside most of what Western society has ingrained in them since toddlerhood.

Take hiring a surveillance investigator for example:

Society says: Mind your own business.

PI industry says: Find out *everything* you can, even the most personal details. Dig through the trash? Great idea!

Society says: Don't' stare at people.

PI industry says: Not only stare, videotape EVERYTHING! The subject's going to the gym or the beach? Great, so are we!

Society: Be truthful.

PI Industry: Use pretext, subterfuge, and distortion to obtain the required information.

Society: Don't eavesdrop.

PI industry: Yes! Eavesdrop, watch, listen, and then write a ten-page report.

Any jobseeker willing to put aside social norms and behave on the job like a snoop or a sociopath must already have a screw loose, right? The trick is to find those rare souls who have a screw that's *just loose enough* to get the job done, but not <u>too loose</u>.

You want your investigators to be able to deceive-on-demand. But you don't want them deceiving *you*.

Hiring

Choosing the right candidate is difficult enough for ordinary companies in ordinary industries. In the PI field, finding the right candidate is a kind of artistry.

We've had candidates with great educational and employment histories fall flat on their faces when they hit the street. One candidate checked all the correct boxes: a college degree, some experience, and a decent surveillance vehicle. But he was a complete nightmare on the job: He was frequently late to surveillance and was always asking to leave his post early. He set up too far away. He put in minimal effort and achieved zero results.

He did not last long—an expensive mistake.

I've hired people with no college degree and little field experience who turned out to be dream employees. One of my top investigators came from an urban school police department. He was street smart and eager to learn. He actually told us he would be our top gun during his employment interview.

Six months later he was just that—a terrific investigator. And he stayed with us for years.

What I've learned in hiring dozens of investigators over almost twenty years is that degrees and stellar resumes mean very little in this field. Hire for desire, and gauge that desire through the training period and the first months in the field.

Here are some qualities I watch for during the interview-training process, clues that a candidate will do well with us in the long term:

Resilience

I want to know how a person will perform after a major setback. Think: Will this investigator continue to investigate after being personally threatened in a high-crime neighborhood? Because this **will** happen in the field. We always say the true test of a surveillance operative is: Can they function after having the SWAT team lay them out on the sidewalk?

A strange benchmark ... for a crazy industry.

No "Municipal Mindset"

I define the "municipal mindset" as doing a bare minimum or having a "that's not my job" mentality. The phrasing comes from my experiences with municipal agencies—the intentionally discourteous DMV clerk who knowingly allowed you to wait in the wrong line for an hour. Or the lethargic court clerk who's openly offended that you asked him to actually do his job.

Nothing destroys an organization faster than this attitude. Be alert for this mindset when interviewing former law enforcement agents. Typically, they've worked for many years in such environments. A slow, do-nothing bureaucracy can infect a person's work ethic—and there seems to be no cure.

Report writing

I know, the bane of an investigator's existence, right? Nobody enjoys writing reports. But I advise you strongly to get a writing sample before you hire. We can teach a lot of things, but we shouldn't need to teach grammar and punctuation.

I don't expect employees to be John Grishams, but I *do* want them to accurately report what they observed, in clear and precise prose that anyone can understand. Watch out for lazy writers.

In my experience, a lazy report writer will also do shoddy work in other crucial areas.

For us, the ability to write an accurate investigative report with a concise summary is mandatory for hiring.

Firing

Firing an employee is one of the hardest things you will do as an investigative manager. I've fired dozens of people. It's difficult, even soul-crushing at times. I managed to get better at it, but it never really gets easier.

When I started my business, I usually gave struggling employees an opportunity to "turn it around." I tried counseling and monitoring. I tried time and patience. I found that nothing worked— the turn-around *never happened*. In my experience, a bad hire never transforms himself into a good hire. Once I get that gut feeling that someone isn't working out, the story always ends with a termination.

Giving employees a chance to redeem themselves usually makes the firing a little easier for me—I've tried everything, I tell myself. But I wondered whether I am harming my business by not removing problem employees sooner.

Of course, I've never hesitated to fire someone for integrity-related offenses. The real heartburn comes from firing for performance problems—when employees are legitimately trying but simply don't get it. If after many tries they still cannot conduct mobile surveillance, write timely reports, or follow directions, I have no choice but to try someone else.

I hired one investigator who seemed bright enough for the job, but he lacked that killer instinct. He simply did not want to succeed badly enough, and he seemed to lack common sense. The final straw? When I checked on him in the field, I found a large man in a bright-red shirt, looking about as invisible as a major-league mascot through the un-tinted windows of a white compact sedan. (He'd said he was driving an SUV with tinted windows.) There he was, working a million dollar case in what amounted to a fishbowl of a surveillance vehicle, resplendent in his tomato-colored outfit.

I was furious. I fired him the next day. Great guy, lousy surveillance investigator.

I always do an after-action report after terminating an employee, in an attempt to learn where *I* went wrong. What characteristics did I miss during the hiring process or in the field? What signs did I ignore? Did the fired employee have anything in common with other investigators I've fired in the past?

Sometimes there are answers, sometimes not. As I said, there's an artistry to hiring the kinds of hard-working snoops and magician like sneaks who will perform well for your business, in this crazy industry. Eventually, you'll get better at seeing the signs up front that someone isn't a good fit.

And you will also get better at firing people. But it's never stress-free—nor should it be. Making tough choices for your business—choices that affect people's livelihoods—is the heavy price of leadership.

Maguire, Barry "Myths Vs. The reality in the Private Investigations Business." Pursuit Magazine. 27 Mar 2016 Web

When your business grows and trust me it will, you will also need kick ass administrative help. I was fortunate enough to hit the jackpot on my first admin hire. In the early days of your business, I would consider hiring a virtual assistant on fiver or Upwork. You can find very competent people on both platforms. Remember to be very specific as to what roles the assistant will fill. A contract employee is much cheaper than a regular nine to five employees. Be forward thinking as to what the role will be today, six months from now and a year down the road. Good admin staff can save your ass mark my words!

3

Chapter 3-
Sales and Marketing

Please treat sales and marketing with the respect it deserves, its integral to your business growth. If I had to do it over again, I'd like to have offered a partnership to a person with some great sales and marketing training, it is that important. If you are going to hire for sales, the candidate should have well placed contacts in the industry-sector that you have chosen. You don't want to wait around for the sales executive to ramp up a pipeline of prospective client. you'll want them to walk in the door with a few clients already in pocket

Sales and Marketing

Get a professional sales program up and running from the second you start your business, cultivate contacts like a maniac. Did you do a bang-up job on a case? ask your client for a referral or business contact.   Never ever, Never stop marketing your business. Business is going well? that's great now go make that cold call you've been putting off.   Market your business like tonight's dinner counts on it!

A majority of people use these terms (ale and marketing) interchangeably, however, there is a difference. I found one of the best description of marketing at diffen.com, a comparison site, they define marketing as "the systematic planning, implementation and control of business activities to bring buyers and sellers together."

Cold calling – I think everyone hates cold calling, at least at first. You *have* to get proficient at it. Billionaire Mark Cuban strongly suggests reading, cold calling techniques by Stephen Schiffman.

The first goal of your cold calls should be an in-person meeting. If you are in the insurance investigation sector, your usual target is the S.I.U. (special investigator unit) supervisor.   Their canned response typically sends me something in the mail, ugh this is almost always a blow-off. Of course, you'll send them the information but ask for a ten-minute meeting and be specific I can be in your office at 11:00 am Tuesday, May 5, you want to check your schedule? Be persistent but not a pest. If you get turned down, ask is it ok to check back next business quarter? Now you have a base relationship. Try to find out what conferences they attend and have a chat in person, then ask for a meeting. I signed one of my first clients on a fifth effort, I had told myself that this effort would be my last, as it felt that I was simply being ignored. Funny how things work out sometimes.

Networking – Try not to see your fellow PI's as mere competitors, view them as collaborators and sources of referrals. Find a group of trusted PI's where you can give and receive referrals but make sure they have a similar work ethic, technology skills and drive. You can damage your own reputation by pairing with the wrong crew.

Join some local attorney groups.- check out the local bar association, ask which are the best attended groups of meetings. Bring plenty of business cards. The key to being a great networker is to not be viewed as a taker. Try to give before you receive. My favorite question to ask when meeting someone at a networking opportunity is "how would I know if I'm talking your ideal client?' then listen intently. This question shows your interest in them, in their business. The question also gets them talking about their favorite subject, themselves (or their business) It provides a break from having to feed the conversation, a gift for the introverted. Do your best to actually connect people, get out of your comfort zone, you never know where business will come from plus people love to talk with a real PI. I guarantee they will do most of the talking.

Conferences

Try to attend one or two conferences annually they are usually tax deductible and the networking educational opportunities are pure gold. I'd also consider attending business conferences outside of the realm of the investigation. I have attended the INC magazine conference "grow co" several times and they are extremely well run and have top notch speakers such as Mark Cuban and John "Papa John" Schnalter. The grow co conference is usually someplace warm like Nashville Tn, stay out of the honky-tonks at night though, it makes digesting Mr. Cuban's business tips difficult the next morning!

Distance learning

The options for online training are endless these days, sales trining is all over the internet. I've been a fan of Grant Cardone's podcast and he now has Cardone University, a sales instruction site, if you are looking to learn how to navigate the sales world in a more professional manner. I have not purchased anything from Mr. Cardone, but he is a top notch salesman if nothing else. Definitely worth a look!

4

Chapter 4-
Business Administration

Business Administration

As a startup, you will likely want to appear to be a larger, more established business; studies have shown that the general marketplace is more comfortable with larger enterprises. Here are a couple of tips to complete this task, until you actually grow. These options provide a professional image while making your life easier and less expensive.

Websites- Your businesses website is the worlds first impression of your business, studies show that you have about two seconds to make a good impression on the web or they move on, yep its that quick. If consumers see an outdated and poorly constructed site, they simply believe your business is just that...outdated and poorly constructed. Clean crisp and informative and quick to load, that's what people want to see. The client has a problem, does your site indicate you are professional enough to solve it? You better hope so, because you have about three seconds for a potential client to make a decision.

Upwork

You can also find discounted but professional vendors on Upwork. Upwork (formally Elance) is a collaboration site that links those who need jobs done with those who have the technical and business skills to complete the jobs. I've used this site for jobs including website creation to cold calling it's all there and priced by the *specific* job. It's a game-changing resource. Need to a dictation service? Dictate your reports in the evening and have them fully transcribed in your inbox in the morning. Be careful to look for positive reviews from the individual vendors though, also note that some vendors are not native English speakers, so be sure to be clear in your instructions of how you want the tasks delivered.

Here is a blurb from the Upwork website;

A new way of working is born

In response, the two friends created a new web-based platform that brought visibility and trust to remote work. It was so successful the two realized other businesses would also benefit from reliable access to a larger pool of quality talent, while workers would enjoy freedom and flexibility to find jobs online. Together they decided to start a company that would deliver on the promise of this technology.

Fast-forward to today, that technology is the foundation of Upwork — the world's leading freelancing website. With millions of jobs posted on Upwork annually, freelancers are earning more than $1 billion via the site each year and providing companies with over 3,500 skills.

A world of opportunities

Through Upwork businesses get more done, connecting with freelancers to work on projects from web and mobile app development to SEO, social media marketing, content writing, graphic design, admin help and thousands of other projects. Upwork makes it fast, simple, and cost-effective to find, hire, work with, and pay the best professionals anywhere, any time.

Upwork's vision

To connect businesses with great talent to work without limits.

If you use my Upwork recommendation, I just saved you some money... you are Welcome! here is the Site www.upwork.com

Fiver

Fiver is upwards direct competitor you can also contract with independent vendors on this site as well. I am currently gravitating toward fiver as the interface is now, more friendly, also they have a great app. The app allows you to track the jobs you've posted and communicate directly with the vendor.

Davinci Virtual Offices

The entrepreneurs behind this service are geniuses. I had been in business for more than a decade when I realized that I never had a client in my office, not once. The office space we rented was terrific, a prime downtown location. We met with our employees regularly, but we never had clients in our office. We paid $650.00 per month, $7,800.00 annually, a big price for no client visitors. We decided to move to a virtual office. Davinci and similar companies provide their clients with meeting space when required (for an extra fee) and a premier address such as State Street in Boston or Beverly Hills in California. Davinci provides secretary services if needed as a sell. Prices range from $65.00 to $250.00 per month and you can utilize any of the meeting rooms in any city. Check it out, it's worth a look.

Virtual Phone System

Grasshopper

We have used grasshopper for several years. This virtual phone system is perfect for the investigative industry. Phone calls come into an 800 number and are immediately forwarded to whichever phone you choose and what makes it ideal for our industry is that you can designate which employee will receive business calls. A fax number (if you still use one) is also included in the basic price. The service also provides a customizable phone tree for different depart-ments/employees. The services then transfer the calls to the employee's cell phone, allowing for constant business contact. Voicemails are automatically transferred to your email. This service fits seamlessly into our business and I think it will in yours as well.

Factoring

Invoice Financing

If you're contracting with insurance companies you can count on waiting at least thirty days to be paid and that is a best case scenario. In all likelihood, you will be waiting sixty to ninety days to get paid. This is one of the most frustrating parts of this business. You conduct a blockbuster case and everyone celebrates, yet your invoices sit unpaid on the adjuster's desk. This type of delay in getting paid will quickly put a serious crimp in your cash flow. When several invoices are outstanding and payroll is due, you simply won't survive for long. So what to do?

Factor your invoices

Factoring invoices is the same as selling your invoices. The factoring company pays you within days rather than weeks or months. The factoring company takes a percentage, usually between 2% and 5%. The quicker the insurance company (or other clients) pays the invoice the less the factoring company charges you. Most factoring companies will require a certain monthly volume and to have the payment checks mailed directly to their offices. It is best to set this arrangement up prior to beginning work with new insurance or investigative client, as some of your clients may not like this arrangement. The factoring company may also require some type of proof the investigative work was actually requested. You may have to provide an email form with the adjuster/requestor. Some factoring companies may also request/require proof the work was completed. Do not provide your investigative report to the factoring company, all of the information is highly confidential. Keeping all of this in mind, factoring invoices may provide relief to the cash crunch traditional invoicing causes.

Retainers and Contracts

Whenever possible obtain a retainer before you begin work, (not available in the insurance industry sorry) Use those allotted funds as you go during your investigation. You can research and purchase boilerplate retainer agreements online, typically you can alter the retainer agreement, but have an attorney review the document before you use it in your business. Some of the retainers are within a contract for investigative services also available online. Make sure the agreement spells out clearly what happens to unused funds. Getting paid first is the best way to go, make sure you charge enough to finish the job, so you won't have to go back for more money.

Rates

Rates vary widely in the investigative industry depending on your specialty, professional experience and client base. If your focus is on the insurance sector rates usually fall with the $60-80 dollars per hour range. The middle of the pack is probably $75 per hour. We charged $80 per hour as our main focus was long term disability surveillance. Typically long term disability case managers assign three to five days of surveillance at a time. So for a three-day surveillance job, we would usually bill $1920.00. If five-day surveillance was ordered we'd bill $3200.00.

When dealing with insurance companies it is usually best to charge a flat rate fee, as adjusters don't want to track mileage. You need to consider all of your costs before agreeing to a flat fee model. Keep an eye on your database costs, multiple searches can eat through your flat fee profit!

When dealing with attorneys and private clients you can typically charge more. We typically charge attorneys $85 and private clients (domestic surveillance) $90.00. When working with private clients please remember to get paid *first* and do a background check on your potential client. Don't get the idea that attorneys shouldn't have to pay a retainer. I've been stiffed on invoices by several attorneys, let my loss be your gain, get paid first!

5

Chapter 5-
Investigative Products

Here are *some* of the investigative services you can market, most I've sold personally, the others I'm somewhat familiar with. I have omitted some specialities because the niche is so small. Take polygraph examination, for example, great niche, but very small, also I honestly don't know enough about it to speak even somewhat intelligently on the subject. Here are a few that are more in the mainstream.

Surveillance

I've listed this one first because it's the cash cow of the industry. We currently charge $80.00-$90.00 per hour for this service. Long term disability clients typically order three to five days of surveillance per case. That's $1920.00 per three days of billable time. Work a six day week on these cases and that's almost a 4,000 dollar bill out, now imagine having two other staff investigators billing the same amount. A good week's bill outright? It can be lucrative.

Surveillance is also labor intensive, you *earn* that money, make no mistake. Insurance clients are also very fickle and notoriously difficult to keep happy. Surveillance for domestic or matrimonial cases can be equally lucrative. We usually charge $90.00 hourly for this service. Domestic surveillance although lucrative can be a bit soul crushing. If you're successful you're usually delivering devastating news. There are a lot of emotions at play with these cases, hence the higher rate. I'd *strongly* advise working from a retainer on these files. Remember to have the professional discipline for these cases, it's easy to get attached to a client and totally believe their side of the story. In most cases, there is enough fault to go around. Stay focused get paid and move on to the next case.

I am an expert in surveillance, I have conducted/supervised more than 5000 surveillance cases over a twenty-year investigations career. I love surveillance, while simultaneously hating surveillance. Confused? Welcome to the world of private investigation! If you want to be humbled, select surveillance as your speciality. On the other hand, it is lucrative and every day is a new experience. Your driving skills will start to resemble the secret service and you'll have anxiety if you leave the house without your favorite video camera.

Below I've included an article I've had published in Pursuit Magazine in 2016, that provides a good basis for my outlook on surveillance

When it comes to surveillance, there are no guarantees of success.

But there are strategies that can dramatically increase your chances of getting the goods without getting burned.

During a rewarding twenty-year career in the investigation and surveillance industry, I've developed a few cornerstones for success in the field ... via the tried and true method of committing errors. I've made plenty of them, and I've found that there is no better teacher than stinging misadventures.

In those early years, I found myself burned by eighty-year-old claimants, surrounded by a S.W.A.T. team, and being flipped off by an irate subject and her toddler children.

Surveillance is simply Murphy's Law on steroids. Hopefully, the steps to success I've illustrated in this article will keep the S.W.A.T. team away from your surveillance position and minimize Mr. Murphy's cosmic influence on your investigation.

1. Choose your surveillance spot carefully.

Choosing your surveillance location is never as simple as it sounds. Of course, you want an unobstructed view of the subject's home, especially for insurance surveillance. But sometimes, that perfect watching spot, the one that offers a perfect view without attracting too much attention to your parked car, just doesn't exist.

A few tricks: See if there are any houses for sale nearby. Give preference to homes with lockboxes attached—they are usually vacant. Try park in front of a home for sale, and you'll have fewer nosy neighbors trying to look into your vehicle.

It's also helpful to park between two houses. The occupants of each will most likely assume you're parked at their neighbor's house.

Neighborhoods have their own personalities. Try to figure out the neighborhood dynamics quickly. Keep in mind that what appears to be a perfect surveillance position at 6:30 am may turn into a school bus stop at 7:30 am. That's why it pays to do your homework in the days before you begin surveillance.

2. Pick the right surveillance vehicle.

Here's a firm rule: You cannot rise to greatness in the surveillance industry without the proper surveillance vehicle. Your goal, after all, is to blend in, not stand out. I've known many skilled investigators who undermine their efforts by using the wrong vehicle on surveillance.

Let's be honest: Some of us hail from a law enforcement background (or have long dreamed of wearing a blue uniform). If that's you, know this: Sitting in aChevy Malibu, or worse, a Ford Taurus, bristling with antennas and with windows so darkly tinted that you could grow mushrooms inside, is simply counterproductive, bordering on silly. The best surveillance vehicles are not memorable and do not in any way call to mind a poorly-camouflaged, unmarked police car.

If you are a true surveillance operative, you will willingly surrender the joy of owning a "cool car" for the joy of succeeding at surveillance.

I'm sorry ladies and gents, but the bitter reality is: You should get a "mom van." The fact is, a minivan is ubiquitous and immensely forgettable. A minivan with a comprehensive curtain system in the rear is one of the best surveillance vehicles there is, bar none, period, full stop.

I have conducted and/or supervised more than 5,000 surveillance cases to date (many of them related to insurance fraud) and have found the minivan to be the stealth bomber of the industry. Choose dark colors, while avoiding red and white vans. Please remember to always shoot video from the protection of the tinted rear glass. I have watched investigators spend thirty thousand dollars on a van, then shoot video sitting in the front seat. Use the tinted windows you paid for!

The next best option to the minivan is the SUV with rear tinted windows. I've used these as rentals on travel cases with good results. The downside is that you've got to climb over the console to get to the rear seats—no easy feat if you're a large-sized person.

I have owned four Dodge Caravans—definitely not cool, but supremely effective. If you are a true surveillance operative, you will willingly surrender the joy of owning a "cool car" for the joy of succeeding at surveillance. Trying to photograph people from a un-tinted sedan makes you approximately as visible as a goldfish in a glass bowl. Get the correct vehicle and be a professional.

3. Study your subject thoroughly.

Don't rely on the client to volunteer the information you'll need about your subject; interview them exhaustively. Ask your client/adjuster where the subject's primary care physician is located, even if there are no scheduled appointments. Obtain a driver's license photo and all prior surveillance reports, if possible. Conduct a national database search and note the addresses of nearby relatives. Hopefully, your database provider has current motor vehicle data for your subject.

If no vehicles are found registered to your subject, run a separate search on the spouse. This may let you know which vehicle the subject uses. Having confirmed vehicle data is a huge edge in the surveillance game.

4. Pay attention to social media.

At my investigations company, we find that a little digging into a subject's social media accounts can turn up extremely valuable information. In one recent case, we were able to confirm the vehicle used by, but not registered to, the subject. The free search also revealed that the subject enjoyed competing in gruelling Spartan races.

We obtained photos of past races and information on an upcoming race where you guessed it we had two investigators shooting video at various points during the event. These photographs decidedly contradicted the subject's injury/disability claim.

In other cases, we've also discovered an incarcerated subject (client stopped benefits), new addresses, and even a video posted to Facebook advertising a subject's new bartending job. Social media can be a gold mine of information that will focus your surveillance efforts—get your mining helmet on!

5. Notify police where you'll be working.

After training field investigators, I let them decide whether to notify local police when they're on a surveillance job. My staff usually chooses to check in with the authorities prior to surveillance. One exception: In very small towns, where everyone knows what the neighbors are up to, providing information to law enforcement can backfire.

Checking in with the police in any location can be a double-edged sword. I've had cases where the police offered us crucial information about our subject. I've also had cases where the police told the subject and neighbors exactly what we were doing.

Generally, I've found it more beneficial than not to check in. It can save you the trouble of unpleasant police encounters. If you do decide to notify police, please remember to never provide the subject's identity or residence. We usually offer a vague location, such as the five hundred blocks of Main Street, etc.

A time-saving tip when checking in with authorities: Have a photocopy of your ID with cell number and vehicle information ready for the dispatcher/desk officer. Trust me: You'll be on your way much quicker if you don't have to ask them to warm up the copier.

If you follow these simple guidelines, I sincerely believe that your surveillance results will drastically improve. Happy hunting!

Maguire, Barry "Five Keys to a Successful Surveillance." Pursuit Magazine 22 Jun. 2016 Web

Background Investigations

Background investigations are probably the second most purchased investigative product (just after surveillance). I've always enjoyed background investigations, they are a puzzle you assemble and sell. Typically most background investigations start with a criminal records check and can proceed to educational and work history.   Use your favorite database provider as a starting point on background investigations. Try to be very specific in identifying exactly what your client wants, then over deliver. During one case I was hired to search and obtain all civil court records for an individual who was up for substantial promotion in the public sector. While at the courthouse I also conducted a criminal records search (while standing at the same computer) The subject had been convicted of embezzlement seven years prior, my client was ecstatic and what was the cost to my company?   Nothing, I was searching the name anyway and just moved a computer mouse. Happy client + good report = more business. Make sure exactly what your client wants before you quote a generic price, their needs and budgets vary. I've conducted in-depth background checks were I conducted in-person interviews with the subject's elementary and high school teachers, then every employer they have ever had, alternatively, I've had the more typical criminal-civil case background investigations. There is a lot of room to up-sell your client on a deeper dive, just make sure you accurately assess their needs. Then knock it out of the park!

Tip: When retrieving public records for clients make it your policy to obtain and copy *all* of the information contained within the file. This will save you time as clients will frequently ask you for more information within the file, just copy all of it the first time. Then bill them accordingly. The invoice will be higher and you won't have to return to the courthouse (that's a major score folks!)

Business Background Investigations

I love business investigations, you'll never know where they will take you. A prime source of business for these types of investigation is the banking -investment industry. They are required by law to conduct background investigations on certain vendors which will have access to client financial data. I recently conducted a multi-subject background investigation of the entire board of a computer database company, that was hired to update systems in a well known New York City bank. Five subjects in all, criminal civil, past business dealings, tax liens, assets the works. I made thousands and never left my desk. Like I said I love business investigations!

Tip: Corporations-Businesses are the second most frequent asset you will come across (after real estate) make sure you purchase the book "Business Background Investigations" by Cynthia Hethington. Some great ideas on compiling reports and client interaction, no need to reinvent the wheel, stand on the shoulders of those who went before you!

Asset Investigations

The majority of asset investigations can be done online, start with your preferred database provider and proceed from there. Double check all data and use a hold harmless disclaimer in your report, some of the data you'll come across is inaccurate, expired or just plain wrong. Double check each asset.

People frequently attempt to hide assets by placing the asset in someone else's name, usually a relative. If something seems off, start with the subject's spouse. Then children and so on.

Real estate is typically the most valuable asset most middle income people acquire, become an expert real estate researcher and you'll do well in asset investigations.

One of the red flags I've come across in twenty years of conducting asset checks is a lack of appropriate assets for one's age and profession. If a subject has a business that is doing even moderately well, a working spouse and is in their 30's or above, they should have some traceable assets. Cars, at least one home, perhaps a vacation spot. If these types of assets don't turn up, there has to be a reason why, find out and you'll be your client's hero.

Computer Forensics

Full disclosure, I've never done a computer forensics investigation, I'm not technically proficient enough. I certainly wish I was though this specialty is absolutely booming; if I could do it all over again *this* would be my specialty. Strongly consider making computer forensics your speciality or partner with someone who is an expert in the field. A P.I. license and a computer forensics certificate can make you a millionaire!

Legal Process Service

Full Disclosure part 2- I have not engaged in process service. I was simply too busy, I wish I had though. I've networked with some process servers, they seem like great investigators. Some have their entire businesses set up around this product, but you have to really hustle to make it work. If your good at locating people and telephone work, this could be the niche for you! This service also opens doors for you to sell other investigative products to your law firm clients.

Counterfeit Goods Investigation

Ok, I've also had no experience with this niche either (what have I been doing with my time?). But, this speciality is also booming and will continue to do so in the future. There are billions of dollars worth of high end knock-off items being shipped into the United States annually. The companies that produce legitimate products are willing to pay a substantial amount to combat this fraud. Sounds interesting and lucrative right? Well, investigate my friend, the riches are in the niches!

6

Chapter 6-
Investigative Reports

Investigative Reports

Reports?? I know the bane of every investigator's existence right? Work a case all day then...the report. Ugh. They are a drag no doubt. Keep in mind though that investigative reports are literally the *voice* of your company. They are read, judged, examined and cross examined. They are vitally important. Reports are also one of the most overlooked instruments of business communication within this industry. Your reports are literally the voice ofyour company.

You cannot be a great investigator who writes a lousy report, you're simply viewed as a lousy investigator. I cannot stress enough the importance of generating a top notch investigative report, put the time in and you will be rewarded, it's that simple. Another strong suggestion I'd make is to go on an e-commerce vendor site like re-work.com and hire a graphic designer to construct a modern report template featuring your business logo and contact information.

Reports are my industry bugaboo can you tell? This business is full of people who write sub-par investigative reports, don't be one of them. Have an attorney or other professional look over your report content and structure, take the criticism and make constant improvements. Believe me, you'll be *light years* ahead of most others in this industry. I've written a well received article for Pursuit Magazine, that outlines my views on report writing. Check it out!

What's the quickest way to set your agency apart? Write reports like a pro.

Here are five easy ways to make your investigative reports the best in the industry.

1. Don't be lazy.

When my company receives prior investigative reports written by other agencies, I frequently encounter problems. Usually, they're the result of laziness.

I recently read a report that was forwarded to us as part of a re-opening of a surveillance case. The video was great—super contradictory to the claim, clear and steady, very impressive.

Then I read the accompanying report.

There was a total of thirty-eight minutes of contradictory video, yet shockingly, there was only one report entry for this activity: It read, "The subject mowed his front lawn." Keep in mind that this was a million-dollar claim for a back and neck injury.

There was no detailed description of the lawn-mowing activity, although the video showed repeated instances of bending and twisting of the torso. The activity should have been broken down into five-minute increments, vividly describing the activity and the range and fluidity of movement.

But that would have taken work, which this national investigative company was not willing to do. Completely unbelievable. Is it any wonder we got the reopen instead of them?

2. Be sure the evidence matches the report.

We have forwarded a report a few years ago, that, at first glance, appeared to be a blockbuster. The report stated that there was an extensive video of the subject conducting what was described as prolonged landscaping in his backyard.

Instant fraud case, right?

Not so fast. In the video, the subject was almost always obscured from view. (This detail was not included in the report.) The only clear, unobscured image of the subject was of him sitting at a table, briefly. But when he was doing yard work, all you could actually see over the privacy fence was the tops of two heads.

In short, the video evidence simply did not match the report. It was inconclusive, and another round of surveillance should have been ordered ... but never was.

This investigative agency wanted to portray a base hit as a home run. But in doing so, they likely damaged their reputation—and possibly, their position on the vendor panel.

Make sure your report accurately matches your video or other evidence.

3. Use active voice, in the past tense.

I have written and read thousands of investigative reports over twenty-year career as a private investigator. There seems to be division in the industry overusing past tense or present tense.

Let's settle this debate: When your clients read your investigative report, the events have already occurred. Writing in the past tense just makes sense.

Make no mistake: Your report is a story, and it should read like one. I have read reports that vacillate between present and past tenses; this is the hallmark of a bad report.

Also, remember to use the active voice rather than the passive voice. What is the difference? I found the perfect explanation at quick and dirtytips.com by "grammar girl" Mignon Fogarty. Active voice: "Steve loves Amy." Steve is the subject of the sentence, and his action is loving Amy.

Passive voice: "Amy is loved by Steve." The sentence gets reversed, and Amy becomes the subject. But she isn't actually doing anything; she's simply the recipient of Steve's love. Steve is the one doing the loving.

The passive sentence does not flow as well. It's unnecessarily complicated and sounds vaguely bureaucratic and stuffy. It utterly fails in its mission of clarity, brevity, and getting to the point.

Keep the tenses and voices uniform throughout all of your reports. They will be much clearer when a judge or hearing officer is evaluating your investigative reports.

4. Include a comprehensive synopsis.

Admit it: Writing reports is a drag. And reading them isn't much better.

Do your clients a favor: Write a brief but comprehensive synopsis. Be simple and clear. If your subject used a cane, say so in the opening of the synopsis. If she demonstrated no outward sign of physical restriction when she unloaded her mammoth BJ's Club shopping cart, say so in the synopsis.

A good synopsis gives your clients the facts right out of the gate. If no contradictory activity is listed, they can simply move on to the next case. They will appreciate your straightforwardness. It saves them time, and that is a courtesy.

5. Write to the target audience.

I was trained to write reports with the audience in mind. As professional investigators, our audience is usually a judge adjuster or attorneys. Write to their professional level, every single time.

A good piece of advice I received when starting out was to write reports like an investigator and review them like an opposing attorney. Look for holes not only in your sentence structure but in your logic. Be clear, precise and — —direct. Remember, you are the one who will defend the report on the stand.

Maguire, Barry "Five Fast Improvements to your Investigative Reports" Pursuit Magazine 20 Jul. 2015 Web

7

Chapter 7-
Database Search Companies

Database Search Companies

As you start your private investigations company you will probably be inundated with solicitations to use one database provider over another, Choose wisely as the price and quality of the data varies. We have used several of the major database companies. Selecting a provider is based on some trial and error, therefore take advantage of free trials. Some of the smaller data brokers provide great service and can fil more specific niches as needed. Here are our reviews of the services we have used.

IRB Search – IRB, in my opinion, is the top of the pile in the database industry. We have used IRB for more than a decade. During that time I have been very pleased with their customer service and more importantly the data that they provide. They added the driver's license and motor vehicle registration information some years ago. The addition of that data made IRB our primary information source. Having verifiable motor vehicle data makes surveillance work a bit less difficult. IRB also provides a tracking feature that allows investigators to monitor when or if a target pops up in a different location.   The asset location database on IRB is also the best we have come across.

If you are starting a new agency, start with IRB.

Tip – Save IRB reports as a PDF, you can scan results directly into your report.

Locate Plus – We had subscribed to locate plus for several years. The data is fresh and they also provide an accurate driver and motor vehicle information. Depending on how many searches you run per month you may want to consider this company as your primary data source. They charged $44.00 per month for unlimited searches. Check it out. The only downside is I think the sign-up process was a bit cumbersome.

TLO – We subscribed to this source for a short time. The data was excellent and the pricing was decent, however around this time the company was sold and the new owners began limiting data licensed investigator could utilize, because of the setup of their home or corporate offices. I ended up cancelling my subscription to this service, as did many other investigative companies. TLO seemed not to understand that all of our businesses were going to the cloud and where an investigator physically worked was almost meaningless. This issue may have resolved itself, but we never returned as customers. The data was fresh and the reports were very good. Some investigators love this service. Make your own call on this one.

Clear – this is a relatively new source in comparison with IRB and the others. We have not tried clear as of yet. I have heard great things about their data. Clear does a heavy volume with federal and state law enforcement agencies. The police I've talked to about the service swear by it. I know that the cost of the service is prohibitive for most small and even mid sized firms. Save this service until you reach "nationwide" status or you can directly pass on the high cost to your clients.

PDJ Services I would also like to provide our readers with the contact information for a company we use pretty frequently. They are not a database provider, more of an information retrieval company. PDJ Services owned by Patrick Baird. They have a wide reach. If you need information and don't know where to turn call P.D.J. if they can't get it no one can (legally at any rate). Their assistance on asset searches alone has made us thousands of dollars over the years. The information they provide is accurate and priced so you don't' take a loss on the case. Check them out! PDJ Services

Warning I also wanted to pass along a warning about companies that claim to provide "nationwide" criminal background check investigations. I don't care what they charge or say, nationwide criminal background checks do not exist. Each state and the federal government have their own rules and regulations as to what the record holder provides and to whom. Some states will provide all criminal data, even traffic tickets to anyone. Some states provide only conviction information. My first starting point on any criminal record investigation is the criminal records manual by facts on demand press. My second step is always the individual states, district and superior court website. Happy Hunting!

Tip: When utilizing a court record retrieval company have them also retrieve records from a person or entity that you KNOW has a paper trail in that jurisdiction. If the retrieval company comes up with no information on either of your searches, something is wrong! This practice is a form of check and balances against laziness or worse!

8

Chapter 8-
Equipment

Technology has drastically changed the investigative industry. The advances in technology enable smaller companies and solo's to effectively compete with more established investigative companies.

A word of advice on technology, embrace the advances in office-based technology (online accounting services, phone systems etc) with as much gusto as you approach the latest covert cameras and tracking devices. Be cognizant of the fact that we all have a James Bond-like fascination with gadgets, just focus on the devices that save time and money!

Equipment

Video Cameras – I've had substantial experience with Panasonic and Sony video cameras and I can say without reservation that I'd recommend Sony cameras. The picture is clear and crisp and optical zoom is fantastic. I currently use the Sony DCR – SX85 with a 70 X zoom. This is an older camera and I am in the process of upgrading to a fully digital Sony (I know I know, I'm late to the digital party)   I have videotaped a lot of fraud with this camera and I'll keep my old friend as a backup camera. It has served me well. I honestly don't think you can go wrong with Sony Products.

Tip; when utilizing your camera's zoom be cognizant of the point where the camera advances from optical zoom to digital zoom. The digital zoom tends to pixelate rather quickly, causing blurry video. I like to use the optical zoom for video and I use the digital zoom as a type of binocular, when not actually taping. Typically the digital zoom is too blurry to pull decent photos from the video. During training, I tell my investigators that if you have to use the digital zoom your stationed too far away!

Still Cameras

We have had great luck with Nikon cameras. We currently use the Nikon D3400 DSLR the price was about 500.00 dollars on Amazon and it came with two lenses. This is an entry level DLSR, but it has been more than enough for our needs. The camera downloads quickly from the memory chip and the photos are clear and crisp. A great choice for still cameras.

Computers

We recently switched over to the IMac. What was I waiting for? The computer is flawless. It's fast and the operating system is intensive. The included video and photo editing program alone is worth the switch from PC. Make the jump, you won't regret it.

Tip – Looking to save cash? look on craigslist for used apple equipment, but be wary some of that merchandise may be stolen!

Covert Cameras

We have had great luck using items from Brickhouse security.com. I've used Brickhouse for years. The prices are excellent and the return policy is pretty lenient, additionally, they will usually walk you through set up etc.

Spy Centre Security (spycentre.com)

Is also a great choice for covert cameras and other gear.

Office Furniture

If you have any sense at all you will buy used office furniture. I purchased used office furniture a decade ago and I'm still using it. Do a google search and buy the furniture locally. This is a no-brainer! Save where you can but invest in a great desk chair, its work the money, trust me.

TIP- Save where you can with furniture, but *invest* in a great desk chair, don't skimp here, your back will thank you!

9

Chapter 9-
Internet Presence

Internet Presence

If you still remember my diatribe from chapter six on investigative reports, you know that reports are my top pet peeve in the industry. A close second are investigators who STILL use a Gmail or yahoo account. Hello, 1998 called and they want their email addresses back! You would not believe the number of investigators I have come across that still have these email accounts! If this is you stop right here and get a domain name email account. Whenever I see an investigator with a Gmail account I immediately think less of them (much less really). It not only demonstrates that you are not fully serious about the profession, it SCREAMS it! Get a professional domain from GoDaddy and have them set up the Microsoft

Outlook email system and be done with it...Whew, I feel better now!

Website

The price of a great website has dropped dramatically however you still need to invest in a kick ass site. You need to focus your web development not only on the website itself but on search engine optimization. SEO will help you land on the first page of results, when potential clients search for investigators in Google, Yahoo or a variety of lesser internet search engines. Make sure your web developer is aware of your SEO strategy before they construct your website. You can also find a contractor on Upwork (Formally Elance). Consumers can pick and choose contractors for literally any business or personal task or job. Utilizing international vendors for some website building tasks, saves a fortune. You can also find someone to do your blog and social media posts...cheap! Check it out before you commit to a local vendor. Upwork

PPC Strategy

Pay per click is a great way to have your ads show up on relevant searches. Have you ever wondered why when you search for lawn mowers you see ads on the page advertising hedge trimmers or grass seed? Well, those companies have paid for some PPC advertising. Would you like your company's ads for background checks to appear when someone searched for a fraud-related news story? Would you like to have your ad for surveillance appear on the page when someone searches for divorce attorneys in your area? Invest in a PPC campaign. Do your research though PPC can be expensive, if done correctly it can bring a stream of steady casework into your office. After conducting your PPC research check out upwork again and review the individuals that are working on that specialty. You can find a great PPC specialist for extreme discounts on this site but again do your research. Upwork

Direct Mail Advertising

Forget it, it's DEAD, focus your advertising dollars on the internet, you can more accurately concentrate on your preferred demographic with SEO, PPC and targeted Facebook ads.

Facebook Ads- This is a game-changer and very few people in the investigation industry (including me) use it! imagine being able to target your ads by income, occupation, geography, or gender? Well that's what Facebook does (and much more) this is currently the best way to segment and target potential customer . Start here when advertising your business, it's cheap targeted and successful. I have purchased a book on the subject and so far it's fantastic. The ultimate guide to Facebook ads

Linkedin-If you are not on Linkedin you are not a professional period full stop. Look at the LinkedIn profiles of those you believe are successful and imitate those profiles. There are also a ton of business article written about constructing a kick-ass profile. One of the best things about LinkedIn is that it levels the playing feels. Small business has access to high-level decision makers.

10

Chapter 10-
Investigative Library

Investigative Library

The best way to get a handle on a new industry or endeavor is to *immerse* yourself in what's going on within that business sector. One of the ways to accomplish this is to read **everything** you can get your hands on. Check out all the blogs, podcasts, magazines and books that your mind can process. When you get cash flowing in, attend some of the industry's best conferences. Here are some of the publications I've used and highly recommend.

The Investigator's Little Black Book

By Robert Scott.

Need an evidence photographer? a private forensic lab? perhaps you need to decipher an employee identification number? This book has it all and more. This paperback is a gold mine. Keep it on your desk. Check it out! Little black book

Business Background Investigations

By Cynithia Hertherington

This book is simply the **best** investigations book I've read. Cynthia also is a featured speaker at several investigator's conferences, she's a professional at the top of her game. This book is a must-have! here's the link. Business Background Investigations

The Sourcebook to Public Information

By BRB publications Inc, Sourcebook Public Records

A valuable resource, a treasure trove of public information. Its an investment trust me.

The Criminal Records Manual

By Derek Hinton

Need to know how the Ohio sexual offender notification system works? Need to find a vendor to retrieve criminal convictions in Idaho? Start here. Criminal Records Manual

Pursuit Magazine

This online magazine is simply fabulous and can be delivered right to your inbox. I really enjoy this publication because it also focusses on small business development and recent investigator experiences. I may be biased on this one, I have written several articles for Pursuit (as presented in this book). Here's the link. Pursuit Magazine

P.I. Magazine

I always get a tingle when I see PI Magazine in the mailbox. There is at least one immediately useful item in each magazine. If your not a subscriber become one...today! PI Magazine

Inc. Magazine

The bible for small business. While there is not much in the way of investigative technique, but you *are* running a small business. I have also attended their renowned conference on business growth, GROW CO. The conference attracts the speakers like Mark Cuban and Norm Brodsky, I've learned a ton at these seminars. Keep in mind conference attendance and transportation are tax deductible! Here is the link Inc.com

Well, everyone, I think this is where I'll wrap it up. If you have learned at least one thing from this book that will save you time and money, then I'll consider my efforts worthwhile! a sincere thank you for giving me your valuable time and attention.